POWER

PRAYING TOGETHER

DISCOVER THE POWER OF AGREEMENT IN PRAYER

POWERFUL PEOPLE PRAYING TOGETHER

DISCOVER THE POWER OF AGREEMENT IN PRAYER

DEBORAH GRANT

© *Copyright 2018 Deborah Grant*

All rights reserved. This book is protected under the copyright laws of the United States of America. No portion of this book may be reproduced in any form, without the written permission of the publisher. Permission granted on request.

Published by: Unlock Publishing House
6715 Suitland Road
Morningside, Maryland 20746
www.unlockpublishinghouse.com
ISBN: 978-0-9991648-5-3

Unless otherwise indicated, Bible quotations are taken from:

New King James Version (NKJV): *Scripture taken from the New King James Version®. Copyright © 1982 by Thomas Nelson. Used by permission. All rights reserved.*

New International Version (NIV): *Holy Bible, New International Version®, NIV® Copyright ©1973, 1978, 1984, 2011 by Biblica, Inc. ® Used by permission. All rights reserved worldwide.*

Living Bible (TLB): *The Living Bible copyright © 1971 by Tyndale House Foundation. Used by permission of Tyndale House Publishers Inc., Carol Stream, Illinois 60188. All rights reserved.* **Amplified Bible (AMP)** *Copyright © 2015 by The Lockman Foundation, La Habra, CA 90631. All rights reserved.*

Amplified Bible (AMPC): Amplified Classic Edition *Copyright © 1954, 1958, 1962, 1964, 1965, 1987 by The Lockman Foundation*

Printed in the United States of America April 2018

DEDICATION

This book is dedicated to my mother in love Doris Grant. She went home to be with the Lord on August 10, 2017. She was a faithful woman of prayer, and she loved the Lord with all of her heart! I really miss you, Mom! Your legacy of loving God and serving others' lives on in all of us!

Table of Contents

Expect Prison Doors to Open! 21

The Manifestation Of The Peace Of God! 24

Illumination To Any Dark Place 27

People Will Arise! 30

Chains Will Fall Off 33

We Are Prepared and Fully Dressed! 35

Access and Open Doors 38

Reflection and Meditation 40

Others Will Desire Prayer 43

Angelic Assistance 47

"Suddenly Results" 51

About The Author 61

ACKNOWLEDGEMENTS

They are always those special people in your life that assist you in making your dreams and visions come through!

I purposely said, "Come through and not come true" because of some significant factors. To birth something out, it takes the assistance of compassionate and concerned people to see and direct what you cannot see in totality, to help you guide it out into manifestation. Between the time of conception and the time of giving birth to the thing that you believe for, there will be seasons and periods of growth and development. However, when it finally comes through, you realize it was worth it all!

I want to thank my awesome husband Donald and our three children, Jada, Donovan, and Nia for their patience and encouragement to me as I worked on completing this book.

Often as a wife, parent, Minister, teacher and friend you have to make the time to do the things that are essential and necessary for fulfilling your purpose from God. My family has thoroughly supported me. They travel with me when I go out to minister. Nia especially accompanies me on my countless trips to the library to write and think. I love you all immensely sincerely!

To my mother, "Nanny" thank you for teaching me the importance of prayer as a young child. It's because of the display of your faith in God, and seeing you in your room always reading the word of God, that I have set my life to live for Him and glorify Him daily! I love and honor you!

To my pastors Dr. Michael and Dr. Dee Dee Freeman! Thank you for teaching me about faith and prayer! I have been serving with you in Ministry now for at least 24 years! You guys have expanded my soul and my capacity to believe and receive everything that the word has promised me! You have given me the tools to launch forth in the Ministry that I'm operating in now! You are fantastic leaders in the body of Christ! I love and honor the both of you!

INTRODUCTION

A prison is defined as a place of confinement or captivity. It is a place or building where people are kept while they are awaiting justice to occur. It is also a place or situation from which one cannot escape without being legally and lawfully released.

We have been called and equipped to unlock prison doors and to set at liberty the captives! We can do it in the spirit realm when we awaken to our role and responsibilities!

1 John 4:17 says "Herein is our love made perfect, that we may have boldness in the Day of Judgment: because as he is, so are we in this world." Our big brother Jesus has passed us the spiritual Paton, and it is our time to run with it!

DISCOVER THE POWER OF AGREEMENT IN PRAYER

Luke 4:18 says "The Spirit of the Lord is upon me, because he hath anointed me to preach the gospel to the poor; he hath sent me to heal the brokenhearted, to preach deliverance to the captives, and recovering of sight to the blind, (to set at liberty them that are bruised,")

Isaiah 61:1 says, "The Spirit of the Lord God is upon me; because the Lord hath anointed me to preach good tidings unto the meek; he hath sent me to bind up the brokenhearted, to proclaim liberty to the captives, and the opening of the prison to them that are bound";

As we can see this was a part of Jesus mission and assignment when he was here on the earth. We are His body and are now representing Him in the earth. This has now become our assignment and mission as well. How do we get involved? Just as the church interceded for Peter when he was in prison, we are to pray for the spiritual release of all of those who are in places of confinement and restriction, otherwise known as prisons. In this book I've taken the account concerning Peter's imprisonment and how the church made intercession for him, to reveal the power that unity, agreement, and oneness in prayer and intercession can bring.

UNITY AND ONENESS

Unity is the state of being in full agreement. It is a condition of harmony. Oneness is the state of being completely united with or a part of something or someone. Jesus conveyed the importance of oneness in the following scriptures.

In John 17:22. "Neither pray I for these alone, but for them also which shall believe on me through their word; That they all may be one; as thou, Father, art in me, and I in thee, that they also may be one of us: that the world may believe that thou hast sent me. And the glory which thou gave me I have given them; that they may be one,

DISCOVER THE POWER OF AGREEMENT IN PRAYER

even as we are one: I in them, and thou in me, that they may be made perfect in one; and that the world may know that thou hast sent me, and hast loved them, as thou hast loved me."

We can see how important oneness is by how many times in Jesus prayer he mentioned it. When powerful people pray together and agree, we become of one mind and one purpose! We form a united chain of an agreement. We then become an unstoppable force in the earth! *Ecclesiastes 4:9 says "Two are better than one; because they have a good reward for their labor. For if they fall, the one will lift up his fellow: but woe to him that is alone when he falls; for he hath not another to help him up. Again, if two lie together, then they have heat: but how can one be warm alone? And if one prevails against him, two shall withstand him; and a threefold cord is not quickly broken."* The devil hates unity and oneness! He knows that

DISCOVER THE POWER OF AGREEMENT IN PRAYER

disagreement, disharmony, and division will stop the forward progress of any endeavor. He desires to isolate and separate us from the fellowship and accountability of others. He knows that a house divided cannot stand! This is why he seeks to cause bitterness, strife, envy, and discord in marriages, families and ultimately the body of Christ. He wants to divide the unity and cause our united prayers of agreement to cease! He hopes that we will never come together, stand on the word of God, and pray fully persuaded in faith because he knows that we will have exactly what God has promised us.

What makes you a powerful person? Take a look at the following scriptures that let you know how powerful you are.

Luke 10:19 says "Behold, I give unto you power to tread on serpents and scorpions, and over all the power of the enemy: and nothing shall by any means hurt you." (We have been authorized and given All power over All of Satan's power)

"God is my strength and power. *And He makes my way perfect." 2 Samuel 22:33*

"Where the word of a king is, there is power: and who may say unto him, what are you doing?" (We are kings and priests unto the Lord) *Ecclesiastes 8:4 KJV*

"Then he called his twelve disciples together, and gave them power and authority over all devils, and to cure diseases." (We are His modern-day disciples) *Luke 9:1 KJV*

"For God hath not given us the spirit of fear; but of power, and of love, and of a sound mind." (He has given us a spirit of power) *2 Timothy 1:7*

DISCOVER THE POWER OF AGREEMENT IN PRAYER

KJV "And he hath on his vesture and on his thigh a name written, KING OF KINGS, AND Lord OF LORDS." Revelation 19:16 KJV (He is the King of Kings)

"1 John 4:17 As He is so are we in this earth. (We are created in His image and likeness. We are speaking spirits)

Each of the scriptures conveys and confirms how very powerful we as children of the Most High God are! We must know whom we are and what we have been charged to do in the earth. In *Genesis 1:28 it's says "And God blessed them, and God said unto them, be fruitful, and multiply, and replenish the earth, and subdue it: and have dominion over the fish of the sea, and over the fowl of the air, and over every living thing that moves upon the earth."* Managing the earth is our responsibility. Many people often make the statement that God needs to do something about all of the bad things that are taking place in our world. As a result, they are sitting back hoping,

DISCOVER THE POWER OF AGREEMENT IN PRAYER

wishing, and waiting with fear and frustration, for God to take over and fix the problems that we encounter daily. Well, that responsibility is ours to fulfill. We have been given the victory over trials and test and temptations, but we must maintain that victory daily! We've been given every tool needed to live victoriously! He has given us His great, matchless name, His unfailing word, His kingly and priestly authority, His powerful blood that purges our conscience from dead works and His Holy Spirit who is the ultimate helper!

We have been given everything that pertains to life and godliness. We have to believe that we are the predicted and predetermined winners by God himself in every area of our lives! When we agree with Him and His plans and purpose for our life, we will see the expected end that He has promised and provided for us!

DISCOVER THE POWER OF AGREEMENT IN PRAYER

Let's look at the account of Peter's imprisonment, and his divinely orchestrated release, and let's see what took place, and what to expect when powerful people pray together!

Chapter One

Powerful People Praying Together Will Cause Prison Doors to Open!

Acts 12:5 Peter was kept in prison, but fervent and persistent prayer for him was being made to God by the church. A prison is a place of confinement and restriction. It's a place where your liberties, freedom, and privileges are taken from you. Prisons can be replicated in many different ways in people's lives. Firstly, there are of course physical prisons, where some that are there have been wrongly or unjustly

DISCOVER THE POWER OF AGREEMENT IN PRAYER

accused and are being held. Then there are emotional and financial prisons where people found themselves enslaved and oppressed as a result of their personal decisions or as the result of the decisions of others that have adversely affected them. The good news is that whichever or whatever types of prison people have found themselves in, our God wants them totally free! However, their freedom often requires the attention and assistance of others to get involved to help them to become free. ***Galatians 5:13 says "For, brethren, ye have been called unto liberty; only use not liberty for an occasion to the flesh, but by love serve one another."*** That is where we come in. We are Gods hands, feet, and mouth in the earth. That is why we are called the body of Christ. In ***Galatians 6:10 it says "As we have therefore opportunity, let us do good unto all men, especially unto them who are of the household of faith."*** We are called to come to the aid of our brothers and sisters in the good fight of faith. We are also here to rescue the lost

DISCOVER THE POWER OF AGREEMENT IN PRAYER

that have been taken captive by the enemy and are being held in prisons of darkness and bondage.

In the book of ***Genesis, he said: "be fruitful, multiply, and subdue the earth." He then said, "let them have the dominion over the earth."*** When he said that, he handed over the charge of the earth unto us, His children. He is counting on us to put things in order, by using the authority that he has given to us. We are here to assist those that are in prison to be set free! ***Galatians 5:1 says, "Freedom is what we have — Christ has set us free! Stand, then, as free people, and do not allow yourselves to become slaves again."*** We must maintain the victory that Christ has obtained for us. We can do that collectively as we come together and pray powerfully!

Are you willing to participate? Can God use you?

Chapter Two

When Powerful People Pray Together, it Causes the Overwhelming Peace of God to Manifest Itself

Acts 12:6 "says "And when Herod would have brought him forth, the same night Peter was sleeping between two soldiers, bound with two chains: and the keepers before the door kept the prison."

This was the night before Peter was to be executed! He was bound with chains by his hands and feet and in between two soldiers that were there to keep watch over him so that he could not escape. Peter wasn't up worrying about the threat of his death, nor was he up crying and upset. Peter knew that he was a child of the most high God. He knew that his God would deliver him.

John 14:27 says "Peace I leave with you, my peace I give unto you: not as the world gives, give I unto you. Let not your heart be troubled, neither let it be afraid."

God's word indeed has a solution to every challenge in life that we will ever face! Peter had a revelation of the peace of God! In resting, he revealed his revelation of this divine promise!

Peter was also the recipient of the effectual, fervent prayers of the righteous, which the word of God tells us makes tremendous power available. Peter experienced the overwhelming peace of God upon him, and he was able to sleep and not allow his heart to be troubled because of his relationship with his Father and because of the powerful

DISCOVER THE POWER OF AGREEMENT IN PRAYER

people praying on his behalf. ***Isaiah 26:3 says that He will keep those in perfect peace all whose minds are stayed on Him!*** When people are in seemingly perishing predicaments, the church must arise and declare the word! It's so easy to become numb to life situations because of the normality of hearing bad news. But no child of God! We should never become acquainted with hearing bad news! It should always cause a righteous indignation on the inside of us that pushes us to prayer and action! We are the answer in the earth, not the government! Let us come together and pray so that the church will experience God's overwhelming peace in the midst of every storm! The word also tells us to boldly speak peace be still to the trial or storm, knowing that It must obey us, just as it obeyed Jesus!

Chapter Three

When Powerful People Pray Together, Expect The Light of the Word of God to Bring Illumination to Any Dark Place in Your Life

Acts 12:7 "And, behold, the angel of the Lord came upon him, and a light shined in the prison: and he smote Peter on the side, and raised him up, saying, Arise up quickly. And his chains fell off from his hands."

DISCOVER THE POWER OF AGREEMENT IN PRAYER

The angel shining the light was so Peter could see properly how to exit the prison.

Psalms 119:105 says, "Thy word is a lamp unto my feet, and a light unto my path."

Often when people are in darkness, they think they know where they are going! They believe they have enough experience and familiarity with certain issues that they don't need any assistance from others and even God. We know that is a form of deception from the enemy, to blind the minds of people to cause them to reject truth from God's word. When powerful people pray we cause the light of the word of a God to shine in their hearts and open them up to receive the truth of the word of God. Which is how much He loves them and has forgiven them of their sins, and how he wants to have a daily conversation with them. When we pray for others, it is so that they can become free from the prison that has held them, and experience the fee flowing favor and goodness of our God! ***John 8:32 says "And ye shall know the truth, and the truth (you know) shall make you free." The light of the word shines forth as a result of the prayers of powerful people!***

Chapter Four

When Powerful People Pray Together, it Causes People to Arise!

Acts 12:7 And, behold, the angel of the Lord came upon him, and a light shined in the prison: and he smote Peter on the side, and raised him up, saying, Arise up quickly. And his chains fell off from his hands."

The word Arise means to change your present posture and position. When powerful people pray, we can break spirits of oppression and depression! The word oppresses means to push down, to weigh down, or suppress. Our faith-filled,

DISCOVER THE POWER OF AGREEMENT IN PRAYER

word-centered prayers will annihilate the strategies of the enemy against those that he desires to devour. In the account of Peter0000, the angel told him to arise up quickly! It is our consistency and persistence in prayer that awakens the urgency to obey God, on the inside of those who we are praying for. The enemy is a master deceiver. He is always whispering in the ears of people to put off or delay having a fruitful relationship with a God! He blinds the mind of those who don't believe. He hinders the truth of the word by pointing out the flaws of the leaders who teach and preach the word and those who profess to be Christian's who continue to miss the mark of living their best life in Christ. He tries to admonish people to get themselves together first before they come to our loving savior so that they are not phony as others who attend churches are. Well, I've come to realize that if we could get our own selves together without God, then we wouldn't need him as Lord and Savior of our lives. So as the angel told Peter to "Arise and get up quickly." We too must know that time is of the essence. We must pray for people to hear and promptly obey His promptings and instructions daily so that we are always under His loving protection and perfect will for our lives.

Chapter Five

When Powerful People Pray We Cause Chains to Fall Off!

"And his chains fell off from his hands." Acts 12:7 KJV

Chains represent bondage and restraint. Our prayers cause the power of God to be present to bring deliverance to those that are bound by habits and pain from their past. Immediately after Peter obeyed God, by getting up quickly and not wallowing in the predicament, he was currently facing, the chains that had held him captive, fell off Him!

DISCOVER THE POWER OF AGREEMENT IN PRAYER

Now, remember at the time when these things are taking place that the church was gathered together praying fervently for Peter! He was experiencing the breakthrough he needed because of the willingness and obedience of people who answered the call to pray! Who is it that person in your life that you know that is currently bound by chains of drug addiction, alcohol, pornography, gambling, spirits of perversion, or the such like. Well, guess what? Their story doesn't have to end with a tragedy result or consequence. You can get involved right now in causing the chains to break off their lives. When powerful people pray, the chains of bondage have no options! They must fall off! Greater is He that is in us, than he that is in the world! No chain or stronghold of the enemy is able to remain when powerful people unite in faith and use their God-ordained authority!

Chapter Six

Powerful People Who Pray Must Stay Prepared and Fully Dressed!

"And the angel said unto him, gird thyself, and bind on thy sandals. And so he did. And he saith unto him, cast thy garment about thee, and follow me." Acts 12:8

As people of faith and prayer, we must stay prepared for battle! The best time to prepare for a battle is before you're in a battle! Staying prepared means staying full of the word of God. When Jesus was in the wilderness and being tempted of the enemy, He fought with the word of God! Every time the enemy would say something to him to deflate, derail, or discourage him, he responded with it is written! You could say that it was as if the enemy was sticking him with those words trying to penetrate his mind and ultimately his heart to persuade him to believe differently than what His father had told him. Well, when he was stuck what came out of him was the word of God! He was prepared before the temptation came with the word. He meditated on it, and it became a part of his makeup. I mean he wholeheartedly believed God's word over the lies of the enemy! ***In Ephesians 6:10-18 it tells us to put on the armor of God.*** The armor is the covering that protects you from the blows of the enemy. Every area of the soldier was covered. In the time of battle or attack, the soldier cannot be in the process of getting dressed! He must stay dressed so that he is always battle ready. The angel told Peter to gird thyself, which meant to get dressed and follow me. Let me

DISCOVER THE POWER OF AGREEMENT IN PRAYER

point out that the angel told him to gird or dress himself. So often, we want other people to dress us. Meaning we always want someone to study and pray for us, but here we see the angel did not dress Peter. God is not going to do for you what you can do for yourself! You are a powerful person, and you have the wherewithal to dress yourself with the word and speak the word to yourself to encourage yourself! God is depending on you being dressed and ready to assist him to bring to pass His will in the earth!

Chapter Seven

Powerful People Will Experience Access and Open Doors!

"When they were past the first and the second ward, they came unto the iron gate that leadeth unto the city; which opened to them of his own accord: and they went out, and passed on through one street; and forthwith the angel departed from him." Acts 12:10

As Peter followed the angel out of the prison when he came to the Iron Gate, it opened on its own accord. It

DISCOVER THE POWER OF AGREEMENT IN PRAYER

opened without human toil or effort! When powerful people pray we cause doors that were once unable to be opened, or that were said to be locked permanently to spring open! That's right our faith unlocks prison doors! Our faith unlocks doors for us that others couldn't open.

The favor of God encompasses the righteous as a shield! That means that instead of people seeing you, instead, they will see the support of God that is upon you. When they would want to say no to you, they would not be able to say no to the favor of God that is upon you! Doors will open for you, and those that you're praying for as a witness and testimony to our great God! Get ready (literally) for open doors!

Chapter Eight

Powerful People Take Time to Reflect and Meditate

"And when Peter was come to himself, he said, Now I know of a surety, that the Lord hath sent his angel, and hath delivered me out of the hand of Herod, and from all the expectation of the people of the Jews." Acts 12:11

Once Peter settled himself down and began to reflect on the things that had taken place, he concluded that the Lord had gotten him the victory over his present situation!

DISCOVER THE POWER OF AGREEMENT IN PRAYER

Powerful people make time for reflection and meditation. We must clear out minds and lives of clutter. Those things come in, crowd out the word, and cause it not to produce fruit in our lives. Meditation will create images of victory inside our spirits. It's like previewing a coming attraction. This is important for people of prayer to practice daily! When you are constantly seeing images of darkness and defeat on the news on a daily basis, you must know how to gather yourself and see a different result or outcome! Meditation on the word of God will cause you to wash your brain so to speak and clear your mind so that you can receive God thoughts and God images of His promises coming to pass for yourself and others that you are praying for. ***Isaiah 26:3 says that God will keep you in perfect peace as you keep your mind stayed on Him.*** You cannot effectively pray for others when you are not at peace. Reflection and meditation on the word of God on the goodness and faithfulness of God will cause you to see what

DISCOVER THE POWER OF AGREEMENT IN PRAYER

He sees concerning you! ***Jeremiah 29:11 says I know the thoughts and plans that I have for you says the Lord, thoughts of peace and not of evil, to bring you to your expected end.*** Powerful people of prayer are needed by God in this hour to meditate to get in agreement with God and boldly pray His will in the earth!

Chapter Nine

Powerful People of Prayer Will Attract People Who Desire Prayer

Acts 12:12 says "And when he had considered the thing, he came to the house of Mary the mother of John, whose surname was Mark; where many were gathered together praying."

Isn't it ironic that as soon as Peter was released from prison that he went to the house where the powerful people were gathered praying? No doubt, he reflected on the miracle that had just taken place on his behalf and realized that this type

DISCOVER THE POWER OF AGREEMENT IN PRAYER

of breakthrough is usually the result of powerful people praying! People should identify you as a person of prayer and one that gets results! How do you serve your gift or passion of prayer to others? Do you offer to pray for people that share with you a problem, issue, or concern? What is your testimony to prayer and the results that it brings? Prayer should be both our priority and privilege! It is the responsibility of every believer to pray! The Bible says that men should always pray and not to faint or become discouraged. That verse of scripture is saying to us, that the way we often become faint-hearted and discouraged is a result of failing to have a lifestyle of prayer. Prayer allows us to remember that God wants to connect with us and those for whom we pray for. He cares affectionately for us, and He wants to be involved in our situations and circumstances. He can only get involved to the extent that we invite him to have access to our lives. He said in ***Jeremiah 33:3 that when we call upon Him, He will***

DISCOVER THE POWER OF AGREEMENT IN PRAYER

answer us and show us great and mighty things that we don't know. There are hidden answers concerning certain things that only God knows the way out of. There are solutions to problems, certain cures for diseases that our father possesses. He wants to give us the wisdom and insight to solve the issues and come up with solutions that will cause us to experience increase and promotion and to excel in our productivity in life. The only thing stopping us is our willingness to pray, seek His face and then act on what He tells us to do. Powerful people that pray and are possessed with purpose will produce more and have longer lasting fruit to show for it. Whose seeking you out because of the undeniable fruit you have in answered prayer? Does your prayer life create a thirst for others to know God more intimately? When powerful people pray together, we stir each other's faith to believe God for more, and to be available more to Him to be used for His divine purposes! Get around those who fan your flame! Get away from those

DISCOVER THE POWER OF AGREEMENT IN PRAYER

who throw water on your fire! As my young adult children would say, "It's time to check your squad"! Examine who your associates are and determine whether they are adding to your life or subtracting from you! Then let's agree together with other powerful people on the magnificent word of God and see the manifested power that's been promised to us!

Chapter Ten

When Powerful People Pray We Gain The Assistance Of Angels!

When powerful people pray we gain the assistance of angels! *Acts 12:10 says "When they were past the first and the second ward, they came unto the iron gate that leadeth unto the city; which opened to them of his own accord: and they went out, and passed on through one street; and forthwith the angel departed from him."* Peter received angelic assistance to get him out of the prison that he was in. *Hebrews 1:14 says "Are they not all*

DISCOVER THE POWER OF AGREEMENT IN PRAYER

ministering spirits, sent forth to minister for them who shall be heirs of salvation?" Far too many believers have unemployed angels! Angels are awaiting the prayers of powerful people to be released in faith so they can assist the manifestation of those prayers to happen. We see in this verse that when the angel was finished assisting Peter to be released out of prison, he departed from him as it related to that assignment. As long as we give our angels and assignment, they are ready and available to assist us. When powerful people pray we speak and declare the word of God. God then watches over His word to bring it to pass. The angels fight the spiritual battles in the heaven's that would try to hold back or prevent the answer from manifesting. ***Daniel 10:12 says "Then said he unto me, Fear not, Daniel: for from the first day that thou didst set thine heart to understand and to chasten thyself before thy God, thy words were heard, and I am come for***

DISCOVER THE POWER OF AGREEMENT IN PRAYER

withstood me one and twenty days: but, lo, Michael, one of the chief princes, came to help me; and I remained there with the kings of Persia."

Often when people do not receive their answer right away the enemy bombards their minds with fake news! He tells them that the mere fact that it has not manifested yet is evidence that it is not going to happen for them. Again, there are often spiritual battles being fought in the heavenly realm. Our angels are persistent in aiding our prayers to manifest in the earth. Secondly, thoughts of defeat and discouragement are thrown at our minds. Then we often meditate on that thought instead of meditating on what God originally promised us that he would do. We then begin to say things that are contrary to what we believe at the beginning of the faith process. Some negative words that we begin to speak cause our angels to be rerouted with the answer. They can only assist us as we speak words of faith that are in agreement with God's word! When we begin to agree with negative words or feelings like doubt, unbelief, and frustration, consequently we agree with the enemy, who opposes God! Let's use our faith and prayer power to agree with God, not the enemy or the inner me. If the inner me has not been fully persuaded by the word of God on a particular issue, we will begin to lean on our own understanding and the arm of the flesh. Powerful people must watch their words! They understand that they are speaking spirits created after the Image and likeness of their creator God.

Proverbs 18:21 says that death and life are in the power of the tongue.

Psalms 141:3 says "Set a watch, O Lord, before my mouth; keep the door of my lips." Your words carry weight in the earth. So let us watch our words and make sure we are employing our angels to assist us in fulfilling the plan and purpose of God through prayer!

Chapter Eleven

Powerful People That Pray Experience "Suddenly" Results!

Acts 12:13-17 "And as Peter knocked at the door of the gate, a damsel came to hearken, named Rhoda. And when she knew Peter's voice, she opened not the gate for gladness, but ran in, and told how Peter stood before the gate. And they said unto her, Thou art mad. But she constantly affirmed that it was even so. Then said they, it is his angel. But Peter continued knocking: and when they had opened the door, and

DISCOVER THE POWER OF AGREEMENT IN PRAYER

saw him, they were astonished. But he, beckoning unto them with the hand to hold their peace, declared unto them how the Lord had brought him out of the prison. And he said, go shew these things unto James, and to the brethren. And he departed, and went into another place."

When powerful people pray we experience suddenly results! The church was praying fervently for Peter to be released from prison. While they were praying, God heard and answered them and delivered Peter expeditiously! *Isaiah 65:24 says "And it shall come to pass, that before they call, I will answer; and while they are yet speaking, I will hear."* The powerful people praying together experienced this scripture first hand.

It happened so fast that when Peter showed up, they didn't believe that what they had prayed for could have manifested so quickly! The young lady that answered the door whose name was Rhoda didn't even let Peter in due to

DISCOVER THE POWER OF AGREEMENT IN PRAYER

her astonishment of how fast he was released! I believe this is the hour that you and I are living in. ***Amos 9:13 says, "Yes indeed, it won't be long now."*** GOD's Decree. "Things are going to happen so fast your head will swim. You will experience one thing fast and right on the heels of another. It will happen so fast that you won't be able to keep up. Everything will be happening at once—and everywhere you look, blessings! Blessings like wine pouring off the mountains and hills. I will make everything right again for my people Israel: "They'll rebuild their ruined cities. They will plant vineyards and drink good wine. They will work their gardens and eat fresh vegetables. And I'll plant them, plant them on their own land. They'll never again be uprooted from the land I've given them." GOD, your God, says so! Listen you must understand the faith that was being released and the fervency of their prayers that were being lifted up for Peter! This wasn't an ordinary offense and punishment that Peter

DISCOVER THE POWER OF AGREEMENT IN PRAYER

was facing. He was not about to be fined one hundred dollars. No mam, no sir! He was facing execution the next morning! This wasn't something for them to play around with. They had to have some serious saints there that knew and understood the power of prayer and what it can produce! God is looking for people who are serious about taking care of kingdom business! ***2 Chronicles 16: 9 says "For the eyes of the Lord run to and fro throughout the whole earth, to shew himself strong in the behalf of them whose heart is perfect toward him"*** These powerful people came together on one accord with one voice declaring the promises of God concerning His servant! Then suddenly because of this type of agreement and oneness, the angel was released to go in where they could not physically go, and to do what they could not do! ***Psalms 34:7 says, "The angel of the Lord encamped round about them that fear him, and delivered them."*** The angel awoke him of out his peaceful sleep as he rested in faith! He told him to get up

DISCOVER THE POWER OF AGREEMENT IN PRAYER

quickly, get dressed, and his chains fell off! When God gives instructions, our immediate obedience to the voice of God is of the essence! Peter followed the angel to the previously locked gate, which upon their arrival open up its own accord! There are things that have been locked up and kept from us. As children of God, we have been given the keys to unlock those doors and go in to claim or reclaim what is legally ours! Some doors will not open until we walk up to them by faithfully persuaded in what God has said and then they shall open! *Luke 17:14 says "And when he saw them, he said unto them, Go shew yourselves unto the priests. And it came to pass, that, as they went, they were cleansed."* True faith is acting on what you believe! Something powerful happens when we act on what we believed for in prayer!

DISCOVER THE POWER OF AGREEMENT IN PRAYER

This story of Peter's deliverance is such a powerful testament to the magnificent results of powerful people praying together!

Conclusion

Prayer is one of the highest privileges any person can have. It is the mode of exchange and fellowship between man and our source, who is God. To know that God our father who is omnipresent, omniscient, and omnipotent is accessible to us twenty-four hours a day and seven days a week is priceless! However, so many neglect the wisdom, power, and peace that are conversing with Him provide! Prayer is the right, privilege, and responsibility of the believer. It is in prayer that we ask for heaven's invasion upon the earth. Through prayer, we provide our father God, access to the affairs of humankind. The will of God is brought to pass in the earth by the prayers of His children. When we agree with Gods will, which is found in His word, we will then ask according to what He has promised. His desires are our

DISCOVER THE POWER OF AGREEMENT IN PRAYER

desires! In ***John 15: 7 says "But if you remain in me and my words remain in you, you may ask for anything you want, and it will be granted!"*** Isn't that powerful?

He watches over His words to bring them pass. We then agree with others in prayer our prayers become even the more potent and dangerous to the enemy! He has no choice and no options as to whether he will release and relinquish those things that he does not have a right to possess! When we come together and bombard the kingdom of darkness In the Authority of the name of Jesus, we are operating in the oneness that our Lord and Savior prayed for us to become. We enforce His will as His body here on the earth! We are to handle kingdom business on His behalf! Every problem that we face can be addressed and resolved through prayer! The enemy has formed allegiances all over this world consisting of people that agree to operate in wickedness, racial prejudice, acts of violence and

DISCOVER THE POWER OF AGREEMENT IN PRAYER

terrorism! It's time that the church arises and come together, unite our forces, use our spiritual weapons and reclaim all enemy held property and territory for the kingdom of God! Your health, wealth, your loved ones and more will be reclaimed for the kingdom of God! It is our spiritual Inheritance to have the abundant life that Jesus suffered, died, and rose from the grave for us to have! We cannot keep doing life, as usual, being passive and allowing the enemy to run rampant! Are you in? Will you help? Will you participate? Can God count on you to pray? Let's do it! Where there is unity, there is the commanded blessing! Can you stand to be blessed even more? Listen, some Powerful people will be praying together, and we will no longer just quietly blend in, oh no my friends we are about to take over! Let's take it by force together!

About the Author

Deborah Grant is the wife of Elder Donald Grant and the mother of three beautiful children, Jada, Donovan and Nia. She was ordained in ministry in 1993 under the leadership of Dr's. Micheal and Dee Dee Freeman at the Spirit Of Faith Christian Center. She serves on the Pastoral Staff and is the Director of The Intercessory Prayer Ministry. She also serves as an instructor at the Spirit Of Faith Bible Institute, where she assist in the vision of her Pastor in training new ministerial leaders in fulfilling their calling and purpose. She is an accomplished author of now three books. Her first book entitled "Have You Prayed for Your Pastor Lately?" is a book with prayers written to specifically cover Pastors and leaders concerning their vision and assignment. Her second book entitled "Arise And Declare The Word!" speaks to the believers responsibility to speak with their God ordained authority and faith concerning situations and circumstances that they will face in life. She is a powerful teacher of the word of God! Her heart's desire is to see people empowered through the word and to achieve their full potential in life! Minister Grant is also skilled prayer warrior and has served as the lead Intercessor at Spirit Of Faith Christian Center for over 20 years! In 2016 she started and began hosting a weekly prayer conference call, along with a team of intercessors on behalf of the SOFCC Ministry. She is a requested conference speaker that delivers the word with practical application lessons every time! You will be blessed, as you encounter and receive her ministry!